W9-BVJ-039

THE STORY OF THE
COTTON
BOWL

by Dan Myers

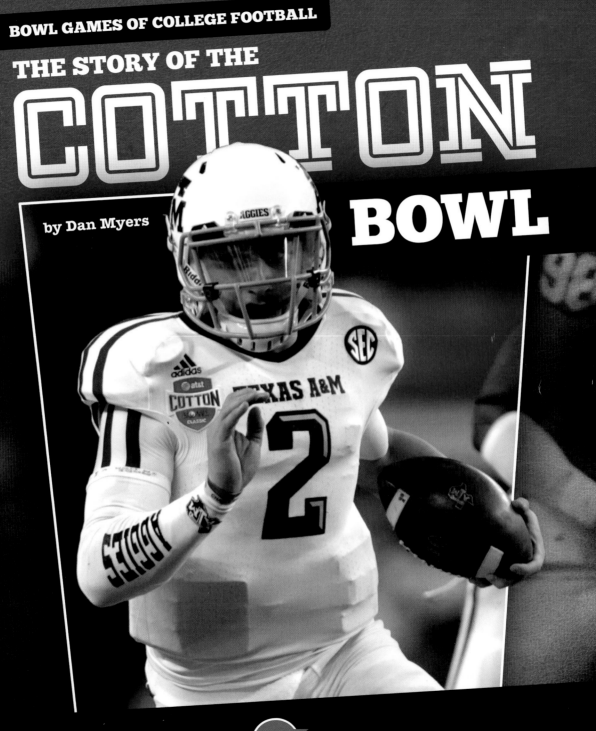

SportsZone
An Imprint of Abdo Publishing | abdopublishing.com

abdopublishing.com

Published by Abdo Publishing, a division of ABDO, PO Box 398166, Minneapolis, Minnesota 55439. Copyright © 2016 by Abdo Consulting Group, Inc. International copyrights reserved in all countries. No part of this book may be reproduced in any form without written permission from the publisher. SportsZone™ is a trademark and logo of Abdo Publishing.

Printed in the United States of America, North Mankato, Minnesota
052015
092015

Cover Photo: LM Otero/AP Images
Interior Photos: LM Otero/AP Images, 1; AP Images, 4, 8, 12, 16, 18, 22, 25, 26, 42; HTW/AP Images, 6; Carl E. Linde/AP Images, 7, 14; JFL/AP Images, 10; Bill Achatz/AP Images, 20; Bill Haber/AP Images, 29; Pete Leabo/AP Images, 30; Eric Gay/AP Images, 32; Louis Deluca/KRT/Newscom, 35, 36; Tony Gutierrez/AP Images, 38, 40, 43

Editor: Patrick Donnelly
Series Designer: Nikki Farinella

Library of Congress Control Number: 2015931362

Cataloging-in-Publication Data
Myers, Dan.
 The story of the Cotton Bowl / Dan Myers.
   p. cm. -- (Bowl games of college football)
Includes bibliographical references and index.
ISBN 978-1-62403-887-7
1. Cotton Bowl (Football game)--History--Juvenile literature. 2. Football--United States--Juvenile literature. 3. College sports--Juvenile literature. I. Title.
796.332--dc23

                                                         2015931362

TABLE OF CONTENTS

Texas players carry coach Darrell Royal off the field in celebration after the Longhorns beat Mississippi 12–7 in the 1962 Cotton Bowl.

COTTON BOWL HISTORY:
SANFORD'S FOLLY SUCCEEDS

New Year's Day 1936 was bright and sunny in Pasadena, California. Football fans from around the country gathered at the Rose Bowl to watch Southern Methodist (SMU) play Stanford.

One of those fans was J. Curtis Sanford. He was a wealthy oil man from Texas. After watching the pageantry on display at the Rose Bowl, Sanford had an idea. He wanted a bowl game to be played in his hometown of Dallas, Texas.

The next year, Sanford made it happen. He spent his own money to create a bowl game. It would be held at Fair Park Stadium on the grounds of the Texas State Fair. No state grew more cotton than Texas did, so Sanford named the game the Cotton Bowl Classic.

The Cotton Bowl parade is a traditional part of the festivities in Dallas.

The stadium was also renamed the Cotton Bowl in the lead-up to the game. But only 17,000 fans attended the first game. Sanford lost a lot of money in the first few years. People began referring to the Cotton Bowl as "Sanford's Folly."

After the 1940 game, Sanford gave control of the game to a group of Dallas business officials. They formed the Cotton Bowl Athletic Association. The group entered into an agreement with the Southwest Conference (SWC). Every year the SWC champion would play in the Cotton Bowl. That relationship ended up lasting more than 50 years. The opponent was usually the runner-up

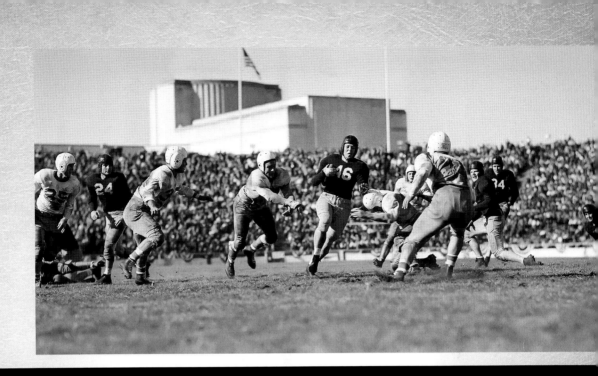

Georgia Tech's R. J. Jordan, 46, breaks through the Texas defensive line at the 1943 Cotton Bowl.

or third-place team from the Southeastern Conference (SEC). Sometimes a major independent program such as Notre Dame played. That system lasted through the 1994 season.

Many great players and great teams played in the Cotton Bowl. For years, it was considered one of the most important bowl games every season. Through 2015 the Texas Longhorns had appeared in the Classic 22 times, more than any other school. Texas A&M had appeared 13 times, and Arkansas had 12 appearances. All three were SWC powers.

Former President Lyndon B. Johnson congratulates Texas quarterback James Street, *left*, and coach Darrell Royal after the Longhorns defeated Notre Dame in the 1970 Cotton Bowl.

But in 1996, the SWC broke up. Several SWC schools joined the Big 12 Conference. Meanwhile, college football adopted the Bowl Championship Series (BCS) to determine its champion. That began a new era for the Cotton Bowl. The BCS chose the Fiesta, Rose, Sugar, and Orange Bowls as its premier games. That reduced the importance of the Cotton Bowl. From 1999 through 2014, the Cotton Bowl hosted a team from the Big 12 every year.

That was not the only change. The Cotton Bowl stadium began to show its age after 73 years of hosting the Classic. So the game was moved from its original location. Now it is held at the home of the Dallas Cowboys of the National Football League (NFL). And in 2014, the new College Football Playoff replaced the BCS. As part of that, the Cotton Bowl regained its status as a major bowl. The Cotton and Peach Bowls joined the four BCS bowls to form a new "Big 6." Two of the six bowls will host a national semifinal playoff game once every three years. Sanford's Folly once again proved its critics wrong.

THE HOUSE THAT DOAK BUILT

The Cotton Bowl Stadium had room for approximately 45,000 fans for the first Classic. Within a decade, that number rose much higher. That was thanks in large part to SMU running back Doak Walker. Fans filled the stadium for SMU's home games to watch the three-time All-American and Dallas native. The Cotton Bowl added an upper deck in time for Walker's junior season. That increased capacity to 67,000. Walker won the Heisman Trophy that year. An additional 8,000 seats were added for his senior season. Local writers called the growing stadium "The House that Doak Built."

TCU quarterback Sammy Baugh was known for his passing abilities, but he also was a shifty runner.

1937
MEYER UPSTAGES SLINGIN' SAMMY

Texas Christian University vs. Marquette

The Cotton Bowl Classic was not an instant success. In fact, it had a rather humble start. In the mid-1930s, bowl games had not yet become a fixture in the college football world. People did not seem interested in J. Curtis Sanford's new game. But Sanford had an idea to boost interest. Texas Christian University (TCU) is located in nearby Fort Worth, Texas. The Horned Frogs had a record of 8-2-2 and had a star quarterback in "Slingin'" Sammy Baugh. So Sanford invited the local team to take part in the first Cotton Bowl.

Their opponent that day was Marquette, a small private college in Milwaukee, Wisconsin. Marquette had never played in a bowl game. But the Golden Avalanche

TCU's Scott McCall, *36*, dodges two Marquette defenders in the 1937 Cotton Bowl.

went 7–1 in 1936 and had beaten some big-name schools. They knocked off Wisconsin in their first game of the season. Marquette went on to beat Kansas State, Michigan State, and Mississippi.

Marquette officials happily accepted the invitation to play in the Cotton Bowl. Coach Frank Murray was eager to expand his recruiting base in the South. High schools there were filled with talented young football players. Murray also hoped to connect with other teams in the area to schedule future games. Sanford kicked in $10,000 to seal the deal for Marquette.

In the 1930s, passing was not as popular in football as it is today. But TCU and Marquette were two of the best passing teams in the country. Halfback Ray Buivid was Marquette's top passer. He finished third in the Heisman Trophy voting and was named to the All-America team that season. For the Horned Frogs, Baugh was a two-time All-American and finished fourth in the Heisman race. Baugh was one of football's first superstars. He was credited with making the forward pass an important part of the game.

As a senior, Baugh completed 104 of 206 passes for 1,196 yards and 12 touchdowns. That might not sound like much by today's standards. But compared with other quarterbacks of his day, Baugh's passing numbers were historic. Back then, it was a big deal if a quarterback completed even half of his passes.

Leading up to the game, one newspaper described Baugh and TCU as "aerial magicians." Fans expected lots of passing and scoring in the first Cotton Bowl. The crowd was not as big as Sanford had hoped. Only 17,000 fans showed up, perhaps scared off by threatening skies.

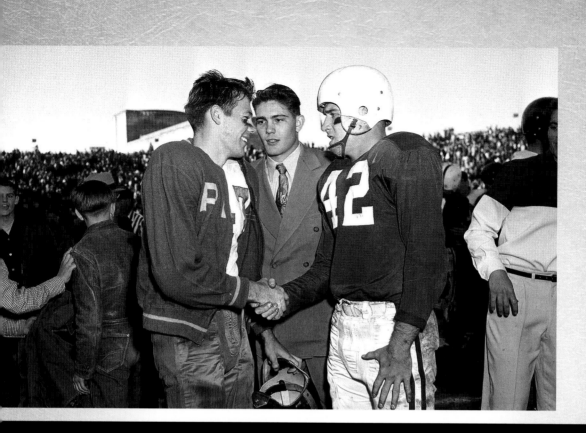

Alabama fullback Tommy Lewis, 42, apologizes to Rice halfback Dicky Moegle after the 1954 Cotton Bowl. Lewis came off the bench to tackle Moegle illegally on a long touchdown run.

But those who braved the weather got the show they were looking for right away.

An interception by Ki Aldrich set up TCU's first score. L. D. Meyer put the Horned Frogs on top with a 33-yard field goal. But Marquette soon struck back. Arthur Guepe scored on a 60-yard punt return to give the Golden Avalanche a 6–3 lead.

The scoring continued as Baugh connected with Meyer on a 55-yard touchdown pass. That put TCU in front 10-6. In the second quarter, Meyer found the end zone again. He scored on an 18-yard pass from halfback Vic Montgomery. TCU took a 16-6 lead into the locker room at halftime.

But the defenses dominated in the second half. Marquette's high-powered passing game fell flat thanks to the dominant play of TCU's defensive line. Buivid completed 9 of 18 passes for 111 yards. Yet he was sacked often and threw three interceptions. Meanwhile, Baugh completed only 5 of 13 passes for 100 yards and was intercepted twice.

Meyer overshadowed Baugh in the first Cotton Bowl. The nephew of TCU coach Dutch Meyer scored all of the Horned Frogs' points in their 16-6 victory. Baugh, Meyer, and Aldrich were named Outstanding Players of the Game.

BAMA'S BENCH TACKLE

One of the most famous plays in college football history took place in the 1954 Cotton Bowl Classic. The game featured Rice and Alabama. Rice halfback Dicky Moegle took a handoff at his own 5-yard line and burst out of the pack. He raced down the sideline, headed for a sure 95-yard touchdown run. But Alabama fullback Tommy Lewis, sitting on the bench, ran onto the field and tackled Moegle just past midfield. The referee awarded Moegle a touchdown, but the "Bench Tackle" was the highlight of the game. "I don't know why I went out there. I've never done anything like that before," Lewis said afterward. "I guess that I was just too full of Alabama."

Bobby Layne was a baby-faced freshman when he won the starting quarterback

1946
LAYNE
LIGHTS IT UP
Texas vs. Missouri

 19-year-old kid became a hometown hero as he put on one of the best shows in Cotton Bowl history in the 1946 Classic.

Bobby Layne spent the majority of his childhood in Fort Worth, a short drive from Dallas. He later moved to Dallas and attended Highland Park High School. There he shared a backfield with another future star, Doak Walker. But while Walker stayed in Dallas to play his college ball at SMU, Layne took his talents south to Austin, home of the University of Texas.

Layne won the starting quarterback job as a freshman, but his legend began to grow when he led the Longhorns to the SWC title as a sophomore. Their reward was a trip back to Layne's hometown. He led the

Bobby Layne shows off the form that made him an all-around star for the Longhorns.

9–1 Longhorns back to Dallas for a Cotton Bowl matchup with Missouri. It was the third Cotton Bowl appearance in four seasons for Texas, and Layne made sure nobody would forget it. Layne had a hand in all 40 points for the Longhorns as they defeated Missouri 40–27.

Texas scored six touchdowns in the game. Layne ran for three of them, passed for two more, and caught another. He also kicked four extra points in a true do-it-all effort.

On the day, Layne completed 11 of 12 passes. His completion percentage of 91.7 percent is a Cotton Bowl record that still stands today. The 40 points scored by

Texas was a Cotton Bowl record that stood until 1975. The 67 combined points were the most until 1979. The teams also combined for 950 total yards.

After the game, as Texas players were getting on their bus to go home, Missouri coach Chauncey Simpson tracked down Layne. Simpson told him, "I never saw a better job by anybody."

Layne would go down as one of the best players in Longhorns history. He set school records for career passing attempts (400), pass completions (210), and passing yards (3,145). Those records lasted nearly 40 years. He also led them to a Sugar Bowl victory in 1948.

After playing 15 professional seasons, primarily for the Detroit Lions, Layne held each of those records in the NFL as well. He was inducted into the Pro Football Hall of Fame in 1967, and into the College Football Hall of Fame one year later. Both the Longhorns and the Lions retired his jersey No. 22.

LONE STAR SWAG

Some bowl games give players gifts as a reward for their season. In recent years, bowls have given players iPads, video game systems, and even laptops. But gifts have not always been that fancy. Before smartphones and computers, Cotton Bowl organizers gave players watches. They also received cowboy hats and belt buckles. While in Dallas, players were entertained by rodeos and enjoyed traditional Texas barbeques.

Navy quarterback Roger Staubach, *left*, talks with head coach Wayne Hardin in 1963, the year Staubach won the Heisman Trophy.

1964
LONGHORNS
STIFLE STAUBACH
Texas vs. Navy

Dallas football fans got a sneak preview of a local legend in the 1964 Cotton Bowl. Roger Staubach would have a long and successful career as the quarterback of the NFL's Dallas Cowboys. But on January 1, 1964, he was the enemy. On that day, Staubach led the Naval Academy against Texas, with more than mere bragging rights at stake.

Texas was undefeated and ranked number one in the nation. Navy came into the game only one spot behind the Longhorns in the polls. The only blemish on the 9–1 Midshipmen's record was a 32–28 loss to SMU in the Cotton Bowl Stadium earlier in the season.

The Heisman Trophy-winning Staubach was the country's best player that year. But Texas was the best

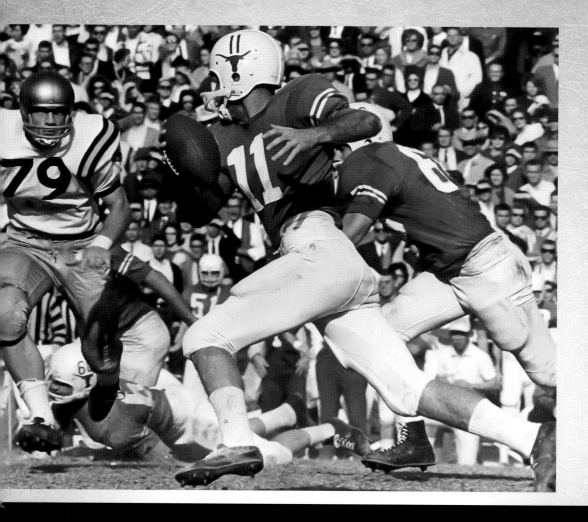

Navy defensive tackle James Freeman, 79, closes in on Texas quarterback Duke Carlisle during the 1964 Cotton Bowl.

team. In those days, the national title was decided by a poll of the media that covered college football. The last vote was taken at the end of the regular season, before any bowl games were played. The Longhorns had already won the national championship. Yet many fans—especially those in the East, where Navy was based—

thought the Midshipmen were better. The Cotton Bowl would let the teams decide it on the field.

It was the first time the Cotton Bowl had featured the top two teams in the country. In fact, it was only the second time the top two teams had squared off in any bowl game.

But that was not the only drama leading up to the game. Only six weeks earlier, President John F. Kennedy had been assassinated in Dallas. Kennedy loved football and was a Navy war hero in World War II. People throughout the United States were sad and angry. Some blamed the officials in Texas, and Dallas in particular, for not doing a better job of protecting the president. In many ways, Navy versus Texas was a grudge match.

It turned out to be a mismatch. The Longhorns raced out to a 21-0 halftime lead. Navy could manage only a Staubach touchdown run early in the fourth quarter. Texas left no doubt that it was the true national champion with a 28-6 blowout victory.

Texas receiver Phil Harris and quarterback Duke Carlisle hooked up for two long touchdowns in the first half. Their first came only six plays into the game. The 58-yard pass gave the Longhorns a 7-0 lead. In the second quarter, Carlisle hit Harris for 63 yards to make it 14–0. Then Carlisle scored on a 9-yard run just before halftime.

Carlisle was no stranger to Cotton Bowl fans. Two years earlier, Carlisle played safety for the Longhorns. He broke up a pass on a big third-down play late in the game to help Texas beat Mississippi 12–7.

At the beginning of the 1963 season, Carlisle was moved to quarterback. The position switch paid off in a big way. He was named the team's Most Valuable Player that season and was also named an outstanding player of the 1964 Cotton Bowl.

HOME COOKING

Since the first Cotton Bowl in January 1937, the game has had a rich history featuring teams from the state of Texas. The Longhorns appeared in the Classic 22 times through 2015, far more than any other school. Texas A&M was second with 13 trips. TCU (six trips), Rice (four), SMU (four), Houston (four), Texas Tech (four), and Baylor (three) are other schools from the Lone Star State to have played in the Cotton Bowl.

The loss was Staubach's second of the season in Dallas. But he would go on to establish himself in the city as one of the greatest quarterbacks of all time. After graduating from the Naval Academy, Staubach fulfilled his five-year military obligation. That included a one-year tour of duty fighting in the Vietnam War (1954–1975).

The Dallas Cowboys selected Staubach in the 1964 NFL Draft. They held his rights until

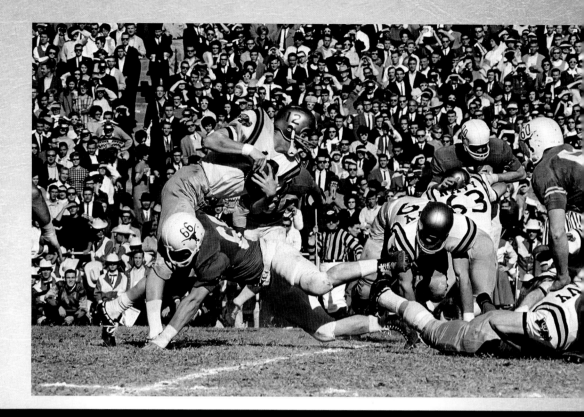

Navy quarterback Roger Staubach, *12*, is brought down by Longhorns defensive lineman George Brucks in the 1964 Cotton Bowl.

his military duties were completed, and he joined the NFL in 1969. Staubach led the Cowboys to four Super Bowls—winning two of them—and was elected to the Pro Football Hall of Fame in 1985.

Houston running back Emmett King, *center*, breaks free from a group of Notre Dame defenders during the 1979 Cotton Bowl.

1979 CHICKEN SOUP SAVES THE DAY

Notre Dame vs. Houston

Perhaps the most famous bowl of chicken soup in history helped save Notre Dame in the 1979 Cotton Bowl. The weather occasionally turns cold and snowy in Dallas. On New Year's Day 1979, it was bitterly cold and windy. The temperature at kickoff was 20 degrees Fahrenheit (−7°C). Strong winds dropped the wind chill to −6 degrees (−21°C). One day earlier, the city was hit with one of the worst ice storms in its history.

Quarterback Joe Montana led the Fighting Irish. One year earlier, he had helped Notre Dame win the national title by crushing Texas 38–10 in the Cotton Bowl. Now Montana led the tenth-ranked Irish against number nine Houston in his final college game.

Notre Dame jumped out to a 12–0 lead on two short touchdown runs, one by Montana. But Houston scored the next 20 points to take a 20–12 lead into halftime.

Things grew worse for Notre Dame when Montana was unable to come out from the locker room after halftime. The star quarterback had the flu, and playing in the wintry weather had dropped his body temperature to 96 degrees (36°C). Humans are supposed to have a body temperature of 98.6 degrees (37°C). Trainers covered Montana with blankets and fed him warm chicken noodle soup.

Meanwhile, the Cougars scored two more touchdowns in the third quarter to take a commanding 34–12 lead. But Montana rallied, and so did the Irish. Feeling well enough to play, Montana returned to the game midway through the final quarter. The Irish were still down 22 points. But then Tony Belden blocked a Houston punt. Steve Cichy returned it 33 yards for a touchdown. Montana connected on a two-point conversion pass to make it 34–20.

Notre Dame's defense held again, and Montana quickly marched the offense down the field. He scored on a 2-yard run. Then he passed for another two-point conversion to pull the Irish within six points with 4:15 to play.

Notre Dame quarterback Joe Montana, *left*, confers with coach Dan Devine during the 1979 Cotton Bowl.

Notre Dame forced another Cougars punt. Montana began another drive. But he fumbled at the Houston 20-yard line, and the defense recovered. The Cougars had the ball with two minutes left in the game. They needed only one first down to close out a win. But Notre Dame's defense held strong for three plays. That forced Houston to make a tough decision on a fourth-and-one. The Cougars went for it, but the Irish defense stuffed running back Emmett King at the line of scrimmage.

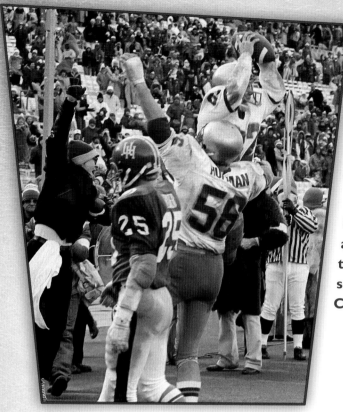

Notre Dame offensive lineman Dave Huffman, 56, lifts wide receiver Kris Haines into the air after Haines scored a touchdown in the final seconds of the 1979 Cotton Bowl.

That gave Montana one more opportunity. The Irish were 29 yards away from the end zone with 28 seconds left on the clock. Montana gained 11 yards with his feet. Then he gained 10 more on a pass to wide receiver Kris Haines. That moved the Irish inside the Houston 10 with six seconds left. An incomplete pass left only two seconds on the clock and one final play for the Irish.

Montana scrambled to his right. He fired a pass toward the front corner of the end zone. Haines made a diving catch near the sideline, and Notre Dame had scored the game-tying touchdown with no time left on the clock. As the Irish lined up for the extra point, one of their linemen flinched. Kicker Joe Unis, a Dallas native, booted the ball through the uprights, but the officials had thrown a penalty flag.

No worries. After backing up 5 yards, Unis did it again. Notre Dame had an improbable 35–34 win.

The game became known as the "Chicken Soup Game." It helped launch Montana's legendary reputation as one of the greatest comeback quarterbacks in history. He earned the nickname "Joe Cool" for his ability to remain calm during big games. In the course of his 15-year career in the NFL, Montana led his teams to 31 comeback wins and four Super Bowl victories. But the 1979 Cotton Bowl was his only comeback fueled by chicken soup.

TWO-WAY WINNER

In the history of the Cotton Bowl, only one player has won the Outstanding Player of the Game award with two different teams. Martin Ruby, a lineman for Texas A&M, first won the award in 1942. Two years later, Ruby won it again while playing for Randolph Field, a team composed of players in the military stationed at an Air Force base in Texas.

Kansas State quarterback Brian Kavanagh, 12, escapes a Brigham Young defender during the 1997 Cotton Bowl.

1997
COUGARS
KEEP WINNING

Kansas State vs. Brigham Young University

The 1997 Cotton Bowl helped usher in a new era with a pair of newcomers to the Classic. The breakup of the SWC in 1996 ended a partnership that dated back to the first Cotton Bowl in 1937. But the Big 12 Conference stepped in to fill the gap. The Big 12 consisted of teams from the old SWC and Big 8 conferences.

In the second year of the new agreement, Kansas State of the Big 12 took on Brigham Young (BYU). Neither school had played in the Cotton Bowl. They were familiar foes, however, having played each other six times between 1963 and 1977. But it had been 19 seasons since their most recent meeting.

The game featured a matchup of one the nation's best passing attacks against one of the toughest pass defenses in the country. BYU's Steve Sarkisian was the top passer in the nation. But he would be challenged by Kansas State's defense, which ranked fourth in the country against the pass.

The game had other interesting storylines, too. BYU was playing its fifteenth game of the season. That set a National Collegiate Athletic Association (NCAA) record for most games played in one year. At 13–1, a win would give the Cougars 14 victories—also an NCAA record.

BYU jumped out to a 5–0 lead in the first quarter. Linebacker Shay Muirbrook sacked Wildcats quarterback Brian Kavanaugh in the end zone for a safety. Ethan Pochman followed with a 39-yard field goal.

The game's first touchdown came out of nowhere on the final play of the first half. With the clock ticking down to zero, Kavanaugh lofted a Hail Mary pass that was batted in the air at the goal line. Andre Anderson made a diving grab for a 41-yard touchdown. After a two-point conversion run, Kansas State led 8–5.

The Wildcats expanded their lead on their first drive of the second half. Kavanaugh hit All-America receiver Kevin Lockett in stride with a perfect pass. Lockett went

BYU tight end Chad Lewis hurdles two Kansas State tacklers during the 1997 Cotton Bowl.

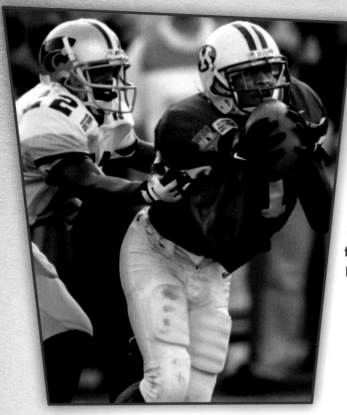

BYU cornerback Omarr Morgan, *right*, makes a key interception in the fourth quarter of the 1997 Cotton Bowl.

72 yards for the touchdown, extending the Wildcats' lead to 15–5.

Kansas State's swarming pass defense held Sarkisian and the Cougars in check until the final quarter. Then BYU's senior quarterback came alive. He hit receiver James Dye with a 32-yard touchdown pass that made it 15–12 with almost 11 minutes to play.

After the teams exchanged punts, Sarkisian led the Cougars on another drive. This time they went 60 yards in five plays. Sarkisian threw a 28-yard touchdown pass to K. O. Kealaluhi that put BYU on top 19–15.

But Kansas State still had nearly four minutes left. Led by Kavanaugh and Lockett, the Wildcats marched back down the field. From the BYU 17, Kavanaugh passed to the back of the end zone. Lockett leaped into the air to grab the ball for what appeared to be the game-winning touchdown. But BYU defensive back Tim McTyer hit Lockett before he landed. Lockett was forced out of bounds before he could get a foot down, so the pass was incomplete.

Four plays later, Kavanaugh threw a pass over the middle. This time BYU cornerback Omarr Morgan intercepted it to end the drive.

Sarkisian took a knee to run out the clock. The Cougars finished the season ranked number five in the country and became the first team to win 14 games in one season in NCAA history.

JOHNNY FOOTBALL

Johnny Manziel had one of the greatest offensive performances in college football history in the 2013 Cotton Bowl. "Johnny Football" had won the Heisman Trophy that year as a freshman. In the Cotton Bowl, he passed for 287 yards and two touchdowns as Texas A&M whipped Oklahoma 41–13. But as well as Manziel threw the ball, his work on the ground may have been even better. Using his terrific speed and shifty moves, Manziel carried 17 times for 229 yards and two more touchdowns. His 516 yards of total offense was a Cotton Bowl record at the time.

Mississippi's Dexter McCluster churns his legs for extra yardage in the 2009 Cotton Bowl.

2009
GOODBYE,
OLD FRIEND

Texas Tech vs. Mississippi

The 2009 Cotton Bowl Classic represented the end of an era. It was the final Classic played at the original Cotton Bowl Stadium, located on the grounds of the Texas State Fair. But before the game moved to the shiny new home of the Dallas Cowboys, Texas Tech and Mississippi gave the old stadium one last memorable game. The scoreboard lit up as the teams put on an offensive show for the ages.

Texas Tech charged ahead in the first quarter. Quarterback Graham Harrell connected on a 35-yard pass with Edward Britton. Less than two minutes later, the Red Raiders doubled their lead when safety Darcel McBath picked off a pass and returned it 45 yards for a touchdown.

Texas Tech quarterback Graham Harrell escapes a tackle while making a long run during the 2009 Cotton Bowl.

Mississippi's offense responded with two quick touchdowns to tie the game. Quarterback Jevan Snead hit tight end Gerald Harris from 8 yards out. Snead then connected with wide receiver Mike Wallace on a 41-yard bomb. But the scoring was just getting started. Harrell and Snead each threw another touchdown pass before halftime. Then Joshua Shene's 27-yard field goal gave Mississippi a 24–21 lead at the break.

The Rebels started to pull away in the third quarter. Just after halftime, cornerback Marshay Green returned an interception 65 yards for a score. Running back Brandon Bolden then rumbled 17 yards for a touchdown. Mississippi led 38–21, a deficit the Red Raiders could not overcome.

Harrell threw two touchdown passes in the fourth quarter, but it was too little, too late. Mississippi cruised to a 47–34 win. In a losing effort, Harrell rewrote the record book. His four touchdown passes that day tied the Cotton Bowl record, and his 364 passing yards were a Cotton Bowl record at the time.

After the game, Mississippi coach Houston Nutt said how special it was to win the final Classic in the old Cotton Bowl Stadium. A native of Arkansas and a graduate of Oklahoma State, Nutt grew up with the Cotton Bowl and understood its historical importance.

"The Cotton Bowl is special to me," he told reporters. "I had some concern about how our players would handle this . . . playing in the last [Cotton Bowl] in this stadium. Our players had the time of their lives."

WELCOME BACK

The 1970 Cotton Bowl was Notre Dame's first bowl game in 45 years. After beating Stanford in the 1925 Rose Bowl, the Irish chose not to accept bowl bids. School officials thought their players would miss too much class if they had to travel to a bowl game. Once air travel became more common, Notre Dame lifted its ban.

TIMELINE

1921

State Fair Park in Dallas, Texas, builds a wooden stadium that seats 15,000 spectators for college football games.

1929

Plans are drawn up for a new 80,000-seat Fair Park Stadium on the same site.

1930

Construction of the new stadium, modeled after the Rose Bowl in Pasadena, California, takes four months, but capacity is reduced to 46,200 as a cost-cutting measure.

1930

On October 11, Texas A&M and Tulane play the first game at Fair Park Stadium.

1935

In December J. Curtis Sanford travels to California to watch the Rose Bowl and hatches the idea of holding a bowl game in Dallas.

1936

President Franklin D. Roosevelt addresses more than 50,000 people at the Cotton Bowl during the Texas Centennial Exposition.

1937

Texas Christian University (TCU) defeats Marquette 16–6 on New Year's Day in the first Cotton Bowl.

1946

Texas and Missouri combine for nearly 1,000 yards of total offense and 67 points as the Longhorns defeat the Tigers 40–27 in the tenth Cotton Bowl.

1949

The Cotton Bowl adds an upper deck on the east side of the stadium, increasing capacity to 75,000.

1954

Alabama's Tommy Lewis comes off the bench to tackle Rice running back Dicky Moegle, who is awarded a 95-yard touchdown on the play.

1964

The top two teams in the country play in a bowl game for only the second time in history as Texas tops Navy 28–6.

1982

Alabama plays Texas for the last time with legendary coach Bear Bryant leading the Crimson Tide. The Longhorns score two fourth-quarter touchdowns to pull out a 14–12 victory.

1993

The Cotton Bowl undergoes $11 million worth of renovations, replacing its artificial turf with natural grass.

2009

The final Cotton Bowl Classic is played at its original stadium, as Mississippi defeats Texas Tech 47–34.

2010

The first Cotton Bowl Classic is played at AT&T Stadium in Arlington, Texas. Mississippi defeats Oklahoma State 21–7 in front of 77,928 fans.

2013

Heisman Trophy-winning quarterback Johnny Manziel accounts for 516 total yards in leading Texas A&M to a 41–13 win against Oklahoma.

2015

Baylor quarterback Bryce Petty passes for 550 yards, but Michigan State rallies for three fourth-quarter touchdowns to beat the Bears 42–41.

BOWL RECORDS

Most passing yards
550, Bryce Petty, Baylor vs. Michigan State, 2015

Most passing touchdowns
4, Craig Erickson, Miami vs. Texas, 1991; Graham Harrell, Texas Tech vs. Mississippi, 2009

Most rushing yards
281, Tony Temple, Missouri vs. Arkansas, 2008

Most rushing touchdowns
4, Tony Temple, Missouri vs. Arkansas, 2008

Most receptions
11, Rashaun Woods, Oklahoma State vs. Mississippi, 2004

Most receiving yards
223, Rashaun Woods, Oklahoma State vs. Mississippi, 2004

Most tackles
23, Keith Flowers, TCU vs. Kentucky, 1952

Most sacks
6, Shay Muirbrook, BYU vs. Kansas State, 1997

Most interceptions
3, Jerry Cook, Texas vs. Mississippi, 1962

Most total yards, one team
633, Texas A&M vs. Oklahoma, 2013

Most points scored, one team
55, Southern California vs. Texas Tech, 1995

Fewest total yards, one team
32, Tennessee vs. Texas, 1953

Most appearances
22, Texas

Most victories
11, Texas

*through the 2015 Cotton Bowl

QUOTES AND ANECDOTES

Only two successful field goals were converted during the first 26 years of the Cotton Bowl. L. D. Meyer of TCU made a 33-yard kick in the first Classic in 1937. Five years later, Alabama's George Hecht booted one from 31 yards away. No other kicker would convert a field goal until 1963, when Lynn Amedee of Louisiana State made two in one game.

The Cotton Bowl has seen back-to-back repeat matchups twice in its history. All four games have involved Notre Dame. The Irish played Texas in 1970 and 1971. In 1993 and 1994, Notre Dame played Texas A&M. The Irish went 3–1 in those games.

"I just sat there watching him, thinking, 'Eli Manning is a bad boy.'"—Oklahoma State wide receiver Rashaun Woods, after Manning threw for 259 yards and two touchdowns and ran for another score as Mississippi beat Oklahoma State 31–28 in 2004.

The first press meal served at the Cotton Bowl was in 1946. The game's founder, J. Curtis Sanford, treated media members to a lunch of chicken, fruit, a hard-boiled egg, and cake.

Since 1993, the winner of the Cotton Bowl has received the Field Scovell Trophy. It is named for Field Scovell, who served as chairman of the Cotton Bowl for nearly 40 years. Scovell, known as "Mr. Cotton Bowl," died in 1992.

GLOSSARY

conference

A group of schools that join together to create a league for their sports teams. The Big 12 Conference is an example.

fumble

When a player with the ball loses possession, allowing the defense the opportunity to recover it.

goal line

The edge of the end zone that a player must cross with the ball to score a touchdown.

Heisman Trophy

The award given yearly to the best player in college football.

interception

When a defensive player catches a pass and his team takes possession of the ball.

recruiting

Convincing a high school player to attend a college, usually to play sports.

sack

When the quarterback is tackled behind the line of scrimmage before he can pass the ball.

safety

When a player is tackled in his own end zone, giving the opposing team two points.

two-point conversion

An option for teams that have scored a touchdown to try a running or passing play from the 3-yard line for two points, instead of kicking for one point.

FOR MORE INFORMATION

Further Reading

Anderson, Jameson. *Johnny Manziel*. Minneapolis, MN: Abdo Publishing, 2015.

Howell, Brian. *Notre Dame Fighting Irish*. Minneapolis, MN: Abdo Publishing, 2013.

Roselius, J. Chris. *Texas Longhorns*. Minneapolis, MN: Abdo Publishing, 2013.

Websites

To learn more about Bowl Games of College Football, visit **booklinks.abdopublishing.com**. These links are routinely monitored and updated to provide the most current information available.

Place to Visit

College Football Hall of Fame
250 Marietta Street NW
Atlanta, Georgia 30313
404-880-4800
www.cfbhall.com
This hall of fame and museum highlights the greatest players and moments in the history of college football. Relocated from South Bend, Indiana, in 2014, it includes multiple galleries, a theater, and an interactive area where fans can test their football skills.

INDEX

About the Author

Dan Myers was raised in Eagan, Minnesota, and graduated with a degree in journalism from Minnesota State University. He has covered sports at all levels in the Twin Cities since 2008. In addition to writing, Myers coaches football at East Ridge High School in Woodbury, Minnesota. He and his wife live in Hudson, Wisconsin, with their beagle, Kato.